A CAT CALLED MAX

Max's Old-Fashioned Christmas

Terrance Dicks

Illustrated by Toni Goffe

Piccadilly Press · London

Phototypeset by Goodfellow & Egan, Cambridge CB4 3JD
Printed and bound by WBC Ltd., Bridgend
for the publishers, Piccadilly Press Ltd.,
5 Castle Road, London NW1 8PR

A catalogue record for this book is available
from the British Library.

ISBN 1–85340–236–2

Other titles in the series:
MAGNIFICENT MAX
MAX AND THE QUIZ KIDS
MAJESTIC MAX
MAX'S AMAZING SUMMER
MAX AND THE CAT BURGLAR
MAX AND THE MISSING MEGASTAR

Terrance Dicks lives in North London with his wife and three sons.
He has written numerous children's books including the *David and Goliath*
series for Piccadilly Press. He has also written 'informational humour' books:
Europe United, A Riot of Writers and *Uproar in the House*, all published by
Piccadilly Press.

Toni Goffe lives in Hampshire. He has been writing and
illustrating for many years.

Chapter One

Christmas at the Castle

'Ah, Christmas!' said Max. 'Holly and robins, roast turkey with all the trimmings, blazing log fires, carol singers, crisp white snow drifting silently down . . .'

'Steady on, Max,' said Timmy. 'It doesn't always snow at Christmas.'

Max looked hurt. 'But surely, on all the Christmas cards . . . !'

Timmy's dad looked up from his paper. 'Far as I remember, it never snows at Christmas. After Christmas, yes, when you're tired and broke and fed up. Then all the trains and buses pack up and you get icy slush in your shoes.'

'Well, if Max wants it to snow, it'll probably snow,' said Timmy's mum soothingly.

Timmy grinned, looking at the big black-and-white cat stretched out on the sofa. Max had arrived out of nowhere one dark and stormy night and had simply moved in with Timmy and his family. Max was a very unusual cat with a number of amazing powers. Timmy wasn't sure if they included making it snow, but he wouldn't have been a bit surprised.

'Anyway, we're spending Christmas with Grandma and Grandad this year,' said Timmy's mum.

'Oh no!' said Timmy, before he could

stop himself. 'Why aren't they coming down to us the same as usual?'

His mother gave him a worried look. 'Grandma and Grandad are getting a bit too old to make the journey down to us, so I promised we'd all go up there. I've been putting off telling you to be honest, I knew you'd make a fuss!'

'It's not the grandparents,' said Timmy. 'It's Mudsea!'

Like many retired couples Timmy's grandparents had gone to live in a bungalow by the sea. Unfortunately, Timmy felt they'd chosen the least attractive seaside town on the English coast.

'Mudsea's very nice,' said Timmy's mother.

'It's cold, bleak, windy and depressing,' said Timmy. 'And that's in August! The thought of it in December . . .' He shuddered.

'And there's nothing to do there. The big entertainment's walking along that windy pebble beach to take a look at the council rubbish dump!'

'Samantha likes it,' said Timmy's mum. 'I told her this afternoon and she was very pleased.'

Samantha was Timmy's baby sister, now having her afternoon nap.

'Well, of course Sam likes it,' said Timmy. 'She knows very well the grandparents will spend all Christmas cooing over her, stuffing her with sweets and showering her with soft toys.'

'Don't see it matters where you spend Christmas,' grumbled Timmy's dad. 'It's always the same, too much food and drink, too much telly, and the house filled with nut shells, crackers and crumpled wrapping paper.'

'Christmas, humbug!' murmured Max.

'What's that?'

'You remind me of a character in a Christmas book I've been reading. A certain Mr Scrooge!' Max produced a large white card embossed with a golden crest. 'Perhaps I could offer a solution to this little family problem? Timmy and I have received an invitation!'

'Who from?' asked Timmy.

'You remember a little mystery concerning the Royal Corgis?'

Timmy's mum looked at the card. 'Max, it's not from . . .' She was so awestruck she nearly curtseyed to the card.

'No, no,' said Max . 'They always spend Christmas quietly at Sandringham. You remember young Clive Carruthers, Timmy?'

'Master of the Royal Corgis? I should think I do. You saved his neck by finding them when they all went missing.'

'Apparently Clive told the whole story to his father, Lord Carruthers. And Lord Carruthers has invited us both to spend Christmas with him at Carruthers Castle.'

'Can I go?' asked Timmy excitedly. 'Can I? The grandparents won't mind. It's Sam they really want to see. And you and Dad can have a nice quiet Christmas without worrying about me feeling fed-up.' Parents being parents, it look a lot more talking over, but eventually Mr and Mrs Tompkins agreed.

A few days later it was Christmas Eve – and Timmy and Max were on their way to spend Christmas at Carruthers Castle. If Timmy had only known what a terrifying time he was in for, he might not have been quite so keen.

'This seems to be it,' said Timmy, looking out of the window of the little train. 'Carruthers Halt. There's nothing here though, just a station sign and a little platform.'

They got out of the carriage with their suitcases and the little train gave a mournful toot and rattled away, leaving Timmy and Max on the deserted platform. It was icy cold and starting to get dark. Timmy was beginning to wonder if this trip was such a good idea. He could have been eating mince-pies in Mudsea by now. He might be bored, but at least he'd be warm – and full. They went through a gate and found themselves in a lonely country lane.

'Now what?' said Timmy. 'Where's his Lordship's limo?'

'I'm sure we'll be met,' said Max soothingly. 'Ah, listen!'

Timmy listened and heard not the expected sound of a car but a clip-

clopping of horse's hooves. A pony-and-
trap appeared round the bend in the lane.
As it drew closer they saw it was an
ancient contraption, driven by an old
man, and pulled by a very old horse.
It pulled up in front of them.

The driver was muffled up in a long cloak with a hat pulled down over his eyes. 'Mr Max and Master Tompkins, for the Castle?' he said, in a quavering voice.

Behind the driver's seat the cart had a long bench-seat, with just room enough for them both. The driver jumped down and stowed their luggage in the back and they climbed on board.

'You'll find a travelling rug on the seat, gentlemen,' quavered the old fellow, jumping back into the driving seat.

Max and Timmy wrapped themselves in the rug and the cart set off. They trotted along between high hedges for quite a while. It was dark now, but luckily there was a full moon. Then they turned out of the lane, went through an old wooden gate, and began climbing a long winding drive. They were at the bottom of a low hill, and there on the hill top was a massive shape, towers and turrets outlined against the night sky.

'Carruthers Castle, gentlemen,' croaked the driver. 'Not far now.'

Timmy felt something cold on the end of his nose. It was a snowflake! There were more and more of them, drifting silently out of the night sky. And the snow was settling.

'Snow, Max!' whispered Timmy. 'It's going to be an old-fashioned Christmas after all!'

Chapter Two

A Cry of Terror

They pulled up outside the massive metal-studded door of the old castle, and got down from the pony-and-trap. Max stood looking at the driver for a moment. His eyes glowed green and he purred gently to himself. Suddenly the driver's cloak, hat and wig flew away, revealing their young friend Clive Carruthers.

'Thank you, Clive,' said Max. 'A most enjoyable drive!'

'Clive!' said Timmy. 'What are you

12

playing at, dressing up?'

Clive grinned. 'Well, I knew Max wanted an old-fashioned Christmas, and I thought it ought to start with a tottering old retainer meeting you at the station. We're a bit short on tottering old retainers these days, so I thought I'd fill in! I say Max, how'd you know it was me?'

'Body language,' said Max. 'You were a bit too agile loading our luggage and jumping back into the pony-and-trap.'

A young stable-lad appeared, and Clive handed over the pony-and-trap and their luggage. He showed them into a huge stone-flagged hall. 'Come and meet the family.'

At the far end of the Great Hall, a little group of people stood round a blazing log fire. To Timmy's delight there was a big Christmas tree just to the right of the fire.

The people in the hall seemed to be

having a furious argument.

'You can't do it, Carruthers,' someone shouted. 'It's outrageous!' He broke off at the sight of the newcomers.

Clive started making introductions, beginning with a plump motherly-looking lady and a tall white-haired old man. 'This is the Mater and the Pater.' He caught Timmy's baffled look and said, 'Er, Mummy and Daddy. May I introduce Max and his friend Timothy?'

Max bowed. 'Lady Carruthers, Lord Carruthers.'

'We've heard so much about you,' said Lady Carruthers.

'How d'ye do?' rumbled Lord Carruthers. 'Understand you helped out the boy in a tricky situation over those corgis? Very grateful to you. He's a nice lad but no brains you know, no brains at all! Young Roderick here got all those.'

Clive introduced a tall bespectacled young man with a shock of bushy hair. 'This is Young Einstein – alias cousin Roderick, the genius of the family. Computers, and all that. He's staying with us for a while, resting the giant brain. Runs his own outfit, don't you, Rodders?'

'If it survives,' said Roderick. 'Call me Rod.'

'And this is cousin Cecilia,' said Clive turning to a plump little lady in a velvet jacket. 'She's the family historian.'

He turned to the last two guests. One was small with a neatly-trimmed moustache, the other big and burly.

'My uncle, General Montague Carruthers, retired,' said Clive, nodding towards the smaller man, who nodded curtly back. He looked extremely cross, and Timmy realised he was the one who'd

been doing the shouting.

The big man stepped forward and said, 'And I'm second-cousin Sam – Sam Oakroyd, of Oakroyd Industries. I'm not one of your toffs, I'm a plain blunt man and you must take me as you find me.'

'I shall be very happy to do so,' murmured Max. He looked round the circle. 'We seem to have interrupted a family conference.'

Lord Carruthers laughed. 'Family row

more like it! They're all objecting to my
plan for opening the Castle to the public.'

'Not me,' said Rod. 'I'm all for it!'

'Well you're the only one,' said Lord
Carruthers. 'Emily doesn't like the idea.'
He nodded towards his wife. 'And Monty
and Cecilia are positively livid. Even
Sam's against me.'

'Only because I want to buy the place
for my company HQ,' said Sam. 'Touch
of history, give the firm a bit of class.'

The General snorted. 'That's an even more disgraceful idea than opening it up to all comers. Carruthers Castle – a factory!'

'I don't want to sell the place,' said Lord Carruthers. 'I just want to keep it going. But unless I raise some cash . . .'

'Upkeep problems?' said Max sympathetically.

'I should say so! Why, the battlements alone . . .'

'We really mustn't bother our guests with family problems,' said Lady Carruthers firmly. 'We haven't even offered them any refreshments! See to it, will you, Clive?'

Clive served everyone drinks from a trolley – very dry Martini for Max, and a coke for Timmy.

'The Castle costs a fortune to keep up,' said Clive as they sipped their drinks.

'Pater really does need to raise some cash. He hit on the idea of opening it to the public, but the relatives hate the thought of it.'

'It's an offence to all our family traditions,' said Cousin Cecilia in a squeaky voice.

'Quite right,' barked the General. 'Ancestors must be whizzing round in their graves like spinning tops!'

Suddenly they heard a piercing scream and a crash of breaking glass. Max ran towards the sound, Timmy close behind. In the corridor outside the hall they found one of the maids. She was crouched against the wall, white-faced and sobbing, a tray of broken glasses at her feet.

'What's the matter?' asked Timmy. 'What happened?'

The maid, who was very young, could only point.

They all looked, and saw the dark shape of a nun gliding towards them down the corridor. But this was no ordinary nun. Her neck ended abruptly in a jagged stump, and the missing head was tucked under her arm!

Tim gave a gasp of horror, and even Max looked amazed. Then, even as they watched, the ghostly nun made a sharp left turn and walked right through the wall.

The little maid was still sobbing hysterically. Max stared hard at her, green eyes glowing. He purred soothingly. 'Everything's all right now. She's gone. Tell us what happened.'

'It was the Headless Nun. She came out of the wall . . .'

By now the rest of the party had caught up with them.

'The Headless Nun,' squeaked Cousin Cecilia impressively. 'She was beheaded for, er, un-nunlike behaviour when the Castle was first built. Her appearance foretells doom and disaster. She pointed accusingly at Lord Carruthers. 'See what you've done with your mad schemes. You've upset the ancestral ghosts!'

'Gel's hysterical,' snorted Lord Carruthers, who'd arrived too late to see anything. 'She probably imagined it all.'

'I didn't – I saw her,' muttered the

little maid.

Suddenly an enormous 'bong!' echoed down the corridor.

'More ghosts?' asked Timmy nervously.

'It's all right,' said Rod, coming up besides him. 'That was just the dinner gong. Dinner is served in the Dining Hall.'

'Pleased to hear it,' said Timmy. 'Ghosts or no ghosts, I'm starving!'

Chapter Three

The Ghost Walks

The Dining Hall was a smaller version of the Great Hall. There were historic tapestries on the walls, and ornamental shields with crossed swords underneath. A huge log fire was blazing and there was even a Minstrel's Gallery at the far end.

They took their seats at the long oaken table and Timmy looked worriedly at the amazing array of glasses and cutlery.

'Just start at the outside and work inwards,' whispered Max.

Despite his worries, Timmy managed to work his way through soup, a fish course, and an enormous plate of roast beef, roast potatoes and peas. He only just had room for pudding and cheese.

He turned to Rod who was sitting on his other side. 'Have you got many family ghosts then?'

'Lots,' said Rod cheerfully. 'Cecilia has written a little book on them – *Carruthers Castle and its Ghosts*. Headless Nuns, murdered Knights, stalking skeletons . . .'

'Ever seen any of them yourself?'

'Well, no,' admitted Rod. 'But Cecilia seems to think they only walk when they're annoyed – and Lord Carruthers has just announced his opening-the-castle scheme.'

Just as he spoke, all the lights went dim. At the same time, the Minstrel's Gallery lit up with a ghastly glow. Slowly the huge figure of a knight dressed in a suit of black armour appeared at the far end of the gallery. The visor on the helmet was up, revealing that the knight had a black beard and a grumpy expression – possibly because a blood-stained lance was skewering him right through the middle.

Clutching the lance, and giving a series of terrible groans, the knight staggered along the entire length of the Minstrel's Gallery. Then, with a particularly deep and hollow groan he disappeared.

The light in the Gallery faded and the lights came up again. The guests sat looking at each other in stunned silence. Then Cousin Cecilia said excitedly, 'You all saw! That was Sir Carruthers the Black Knight! After a lifetime of black-hearted villainy he rebelled against the King. He was defeated in a joust by the King's Champion. Ever since then he's stalked the Castle, clutching the lance that killed him.'

'I expect he feels sort of attached to it!' whispered Timothy.

'Every time he appears,' continued Cecilia, 'it means –'

'Don't tell me,' interrupted Rod.

'Doom and disaster!'

'Well, he might have the good manners not to appear during dinner,' said Lady Carruthers.

'Quite right,' said Lord Carruthers. 'He should do his haunting at midnight like any respectable ghost!'

Max turned to Clive who was sitting next to him. 'Have you seen any of these family ghosts before tonight?'

'Can't say I have. Nor has anyone else, as far as I know.'

'Well, they're certainly on the move tonight,' said Timmy.

'What are we going to do, Max?'

'I don't really know what one can do about ghosts,' said Max. 'Perhaps they're trying to tell us something . . .'

'Of course they are,' said the General. 'Cecilia's right, they object to this plan to open the Castle to the public.'

'You'd think they'd be glad of a bit of company,' called Sam Oakroyd from the other side of the table. 'They must get pretty bored haunting just you lot!'

'It appears they don't even do that,' said Max. 'Until tonight.' His eyes glowed green and Timmy could see he was thinking hard.

'Coffee will be served in the Great Hall,' called Lady Carruthers. 'After that we shall wait till midnight, and then switch on the Christmas tree lights.'

'Old family custom,' whispered Clive.

'I'd better go and make sure the lights are working,' said Rod. 'I persuaded his Lordship to put me in charge of them this year.' He slipped away from the table.

After dinner everyone gathered in the Great Hall again. Rod was still working on the Christmas tree. By now it was covered with all kinds of decorations including glowing glass spheres in every imaginable colour, and lights made to look exactly like real candles. More drinks were served and everyone chatted excitedly about the ghosts.

'We usually tell ghost stories about this time,' said Clive. 'But with real ghosts around there doesn't seem much point!'

Suddenly the old grandfather clock in the corner whirred and clicked and gave out a rather wheezy 'boinggg!'

'First stroke of midnight,' called Lord Carruthers. 'Ready, Rod?'

As the last 'boingg' died away, the room lights dimmed, Rod flicked a switch and the Christmas tree lit up. The candle-lights were so realistic that they actually flickered like real candles, and the multi-coloured globes glowed softly as well. Everyone clapped.

'A wonderful job, Roderick,' said Lady Carruthers. 'That's quite the best display we've ever had.'

Suddenly the Christmas tree lights started to dim. At the same time, a column of white light appeared in the centre of the room. Inside it a shape was forming – the shape of a giant glowing skeleton . . .

Chapter Four

Max on the Trail

Timmy had to admit that of all the apparitions they'd seen this one was by far the most frightening. The enormous skeleton was crowned by a skull – a skull with glowing red eyes.

The skeleton stalked forward, its bones rattling, great bony hands reaching out . . .

Lady Carruthers screamed . . .

As if the sound broke some spell the skeleton faded and disappeared, and the

Christmas tree lights glowed brightly again. Timmy found his teeth were chattering. 'W-w-what was that?'

'I'm sure Cousin Cecilia can tell us,' said Max. 'I expect our bony friend is in her book with all the others.'

'Most certainly,' said Cecilia. 'That was the ghost of Ivo Carruthers – better known as Ivo the Terrible.'

'Why does he turn up all bone and bone?' asked Timmy.

'Because of the terrible way he died,' said Cecilia. 'Sir Ivo was a cruel master, always ill-treating his servants. And he was terribly fussy about his food. When he sent back the soup for the third time running, his maddened kitchen staff snapped. They seized Sir Ivo and hurled him into the big bubbling soup tureen that hung over the kitchen fire. Frightened at what they had done the kitchen staff fled. In no time at all, Ivo had been boiled away to bones.'

'And there was a soup with plenty of body,' said Timmy.

'Ever since then his ghost has stalked the Castle in the shape of a skeleton,' said Cecilia.

'Quite so,' said Max. 'Needless to say its appearance means –'

'Doom and disaster!' said Cecilia. She turned to Lord Carruthers. 'Surely you'll abandon this mad scheme of yours now?'

'Cousin Cecilia's got a point, Pater,' said Clive. 'I mean, how long would your visitors stay with family ghosts popping up all the time?'

'That's right,' said Sam Oakroyd. 'Folk'll not pay out good brass to be frightened into fits!'

Before Lord Carruthers could reply, Max said smoothly, 'May I suggest that you put off your final decision until tomorrow? I may be able to be of some assistance to you by then. Meanwhile, I wonder if I might use your library?'

'Certainly,' said Lord Carruthers. 'Clive will show you.'

Clive took Max off to the library, and then came back to rejoin the party. Very soon Max returned, looking very pleased with himself.

A maid came in with a steaming bowl of Christmas punch. After a few glasses everyone cheered up immensely. The night ended with them all drinking toasts around the tree and wishing each other happy Christmas.

At the end of the night Clive showed Max and Timmy to their room. Timmy was quite glad to find he was sharing with Max in a twin-bedded room. If he had to spend a night in a haunted castle, he didn't want to do it on his own.

'Well, it certainly hasn't been dull,' said Timmy, as they got ready for bed.

Max put on an elegant nightcap with a tassel on the end. 'Sorry you came, old chap?'

Timmy yawned. 'Not a bit. Beats Christmas telly any day! What were you up to in the library?'

'Oh just a bit of research,' said Max.

'Good night, old fellow.'

After all the fuss Timmy thought he might be too nervous to sleep. But it had been a late night after a long day and he dropped off almost at once. But he didn't sleep for very long. As sometimes happens, he suddenly found himself wide awake in the darkness, without knowing why.

'Max?' he called. 'Max, are you awake?'

There was no reply.

When he was much younger, Timmy had been a bit scared of the dark. He'd cured himself by keeping a little torch under the pillow. If he woke up feeling nervous he could always shine the torch round the room and make sure everything was all right. It was a habit he'd kept up, and fishing out the torch he shone it round the bedroom. But this time everything wasn't all right. Max had disappeared. His nightcap lay on his pillow but there was no Max underneath it.

For a moment Timmy was tempted to pull the covers over his head and go back to sleep, but he knew it wouldn't do. Perhaps Max had been kidnapped by some mysterious ghostly force – or perhaps he'd gone ghost-hunting on his own. In either case, Timmy wanted to know what was going on. Putting on his dressing gown and slippers he went off to look for Max.

He remembered coming up a massive flight of stairs, and along stone-flagged corridors. Shining his torch ahead of him, Timmy went out of the room, and along the corridor, looking for the Great Hall.

It was a spooky journey. The corridor was dark and cold, lit only by the thin beam of Timmy's torch, and it seemed to go on forever. Suddenly a menacing figure loomed up ahead of him – and it was clutching some kind of weapon . . .

Timmy raised the torch beam and gave a sigh of relief. It was only an ornamental suit of armour, battle axe in one metal hand – and it was standing at the head of the stairs. Cautiously Timmy started to descend into the main hall.

Halfway down the stairs he heard a faint tinkling sound. It was coming from the Christmas tree. He crept closer and saw a dark shape examining one of the glass globes. It was Max. He let go of the globe, turned and saw Timmy.

'What are you doing out of bed, dear boy?'

'What about you? Why are you messing about with the tree?'

'Just confirming a theory.'

'What theory?' demanded Timmy. 'What's going on?'

Before Max could answer there was a flash of lightning and the crash of thunder. A giant voice boomed, 'Beware! You have aroused the anger of the ghosts of Carruthers Castle. You are doomed!' A mad peal of ghostly laughter echoed around the Great Hall. The Headless Nun appeared out of the wall on their left.

Head tucked neatly under her arm, she glided towards them . . . A creak of rusty metal came from the right-hand wall, and the Black Knight appeared, still skewered by the lance, and still looking fed up about it.

But the worst was still to come. A column of light appeared in the rear wall and from it stalked forth the giant skeleton, of Sir Ivo the Terrible, bones rattling, teeth chattering, red eyes glowing in the ghastly skull.

Nun, knight and skeleton glided, clanked and stalked towards the Christmas tree – and towards Max and Timmy.

Timmy's teeth were chattering as loudly as the skeleton's. 'Surrounded by ghastly ghosts!' he thought. 'The voice was right. We're doomed!'

But Max wasn't beaten yet. Fearlessly

he confronted the advancing ghosts. He drew himself up to his full height and his eyes glowed green. He began to purr – that deep dynamic purr that always meant something amazing was going to happen – and something did! Max whirled round and turned that green gaze on the Christmas tree. All the lights came on and the coloured globes began glowing brightly. The ghosts suddenly started to flicker in and out of existence. Then they speeded up, like an old film. Then they all rushed forward, colliding in the centre of the room. They began to spin round, a whirling column of light with nun, ghost and skeleton all mixed up together.

Timmy looked at the tree and saw that one globe in particular was glowing brighter than all the others. Suddenly it burst – and the whirling ghosts disappeared.

Max went to a wall-switch and turned on the main lights – revealing the rest of the party, in a variety of nightwear, gathered at the top of the stairs.

'What's going on?' called Lord Carruthers. 'We were all woken up by the confounded noise!'

'That was the ghosts of Carruthers Castle making their final appearance,' said Max. 'At least, for the time being. Come down everyone, and I'll explain . . .'

Chapter Five

Detective Max

'Now then Max,' said Lord Carruthers. 'You promised to explain all these ghostly goings on.'

It was some time later. The fire had been made up and they were all sitting round the blaze, drinking mugs of steaming cocoa. Everyone was there – Timmy and Max, Lord and Lady Carruthers, Rod, Clive, General Carruthers, Sam Oakroyd and Cousin Cecilia. 'Just like the end of an Agatha

Christie mystery,' thought Timmy. 'Any minute now, old Max'll start twirling his moustache and talking about zee little grey cells. . .'

'It was an unusual investigation,' said Max modestly. 'Detection turns on three things, means, motive and opportunity. Let's take them in reverse order.' He twirled his whiskers.

'I knew it!' thought Timmy. 'Zee little grey cells next.'

'Opportunity,' Max continued. 'Timmy and I apart, you'd all been here for some time. Motive – most of you seemed against Lord Carruthers's scheme to open the Castle to visitors. Cousin Cecilia and the General felt it outraged family tradition. Mr Oakroyd wanted the Castle for his HQ.

'I wasn't against it,' protested Clive.
'Nor me,' said Rod.

'Ah,' said Max. 'But as the heir, Clive, you might have been just as outraged as your relatives – and concealing the fact to divert suspicion. And Roderick might be lying too. So, we come down to means. I was pretty sure the ghosts were being faked – look how neatly they turned up on cue. But who would have the skill to do it?' He looked at the General. 'Soldiers sometimes use cunning technical tricks in wartime – but when I looked you up in the Army list, General, I found your entire military career had been in the Catering Corps.'

'Vital service,' said the General. 'Army marches on its stomach.'

'Vital indeed,' agreed Max. 'But not the most hi-tech.'

He turned to Sam Oakroyd. 'An industrial tycoon might have all sorts of technological resources. However, I

looked up Oakroyd Industries in the
Business Guide and found it
manufactured bathroom fittings and
sanitary ware.'

'Cleanliness is next to godlincss,'
rumbled Sam Oakroyd. 'And when
you've got to go, you've got to go.'

'Quite,' said Max hastily. 'But again, scarcely the right kind of technology.' He looked round the circle. 'Cousin Cecilia here knew more about the family ghosts than anyone else.'

Cousin Cecilia suddenly looked worried.

'However, hers was a historian's knowledge,' Max went on. 'I couldn't believe she knew how to produce fake ghosts. Since she'd put her knowledge in a book, it was there for anyone to use.'

Cecilia looked relieved and Max turned to Clive. 'There's my young friend Clive here – but I believe he's pretty non-technical too?'

'Non-brained, you mean,' said Lord Carruthers. 'Wouldn't trust him to change a light bulb, let alone fake a spook.'

'Quite right,' said Clive cheerfully.

'So that lets me off! Helps to be dim sometimes!'

'Well then,' said Max. 'Assuming Lord Carruthers had no motive to sabotage his own plan, and that Lady Carruthers, even if she disapproves would feel it her duty to support him . . .'

By now everyone was looking at Rod, who sat in defiant silence.

'You were introduced to me as "Young Einstein",' murmured Max. 'There was some mention of computers and computers are involved in everything these days.' Max pointed an accusing paw at Rod. 'Lord Carruthers's library contains a Film Yearbook – with an excellent account of your firm's work in computer-enhanced special effects for the movies. Things like dinosaurs – and ghosts, perhaps?'

'All right,' said Rod. 'It's a fair cop.'

'But why?' asked Timmy, feeling like Doctor Watson – or Captain Hastings. All great detectives have to have a resident twit to ask dumb questions and be amazed by their brilliance.

'I wanted the Castle too,' said Rod. 'My firm's doing pioneering work, special effects, holograms, the lot. But times have been hard and London rents are crippling us. I hoped to persuade Lord Carruthers to let me use the Castle as a special effects lab and workshop – rent-free, to be paid for from future profits. I thought if his visitors scheme worked he wouldn't want to know. So I just moved up some of my latest equipment and raised the family ghosts.'

'Holographic projection, I take it?' Max pointed to the shattered globe on the Christmas tree. 'Using the lights, which you'd installed, as control mechanisms!'

'Yes, until you scrambled all my circuits,' said Rod indignantly. 'How did you do that?'

'Classified information,' murmured Max.

'Well, it's all been most interesting,' said Lord Carruthers. 'Never had such an exciting Christmas. But none of this solves my financial problems. I know most of you hate the visitors scheme. But the poor old Castle's falling down, so what do I do?'

Timmy looked at Max. 'I bet you've got a plan, Max!'

'Well,' drawled Max, 'I do have a suggestion, as it happens. You said yourself, Lord Carruthers, you'd never had such an exciting Christmas. And I suspect we've all rather enjoyed ourselves too.' Suddenly Timmy realised Max was right. It had been scary – but it had been fun as well – like a ride on a roller-coaster.

'Mr Oakroyd, a while ago you said people won't pay good money to be frightened into fits,' Max continued. 'But if you think about it, that's exactly what they will pay for! Horror films, theme parks, Haunted Houses, dinosaur films . . .'

'What exactly are you suggesting?'

asked Lady Carruthers.

'Special guest weekends – small select house-parties, once a month. "Dare You Spend A Weekend in a Haunted Castle?" You provide the old-world atmosphere, Rod provides the ghosts. You could give him his workshop space as part of the deal.'

'By heck, you'll make a fortune,' said

Sam Oakroyd. 'And I'll back you too. It'll be a bigger draw than Jurassic Park.'

'Dashed fine idea,' said the General. 'I'll ask some of the chaps at the Club.'

'One weekend a month wouldn't be so bad,' said Cousin Cecilia grudgingly. 'Better than hordes of people tramping about.'

'I'll give 'em ghosts that'll chill their blood,' said Rod happily. 'Once I get those scrambled circuits repaired . . .'

'Well, Max,' said Clive, 'it seems you've saved the Carruthers family fortunes once again. To Max, everyone!'

'No please,' protested Max. 'You make me blush to the roots of my fur! Timmy, you think of a toast for us.'

'We'll have a combined toast,' said Timmy. He raised his cocoa mug. 'To Max – to the ghosts of Carruthers Castle – and to a real old-fashioned Christmas!'